D0955901

DEC 1 4

LOOM
Magic Creatures!

LOOM
Magic Creatures!

25 Awesome Animals and Mythical Beings
for a Rainbow of Critters

Becky Thomas &
Monica Sweeney

Sky Pony Press
New York

Sky Pony Press books may be purchased in bulk at special discounts for sales promotion, corporate gifts, fund-raising, or educational purposes. Special editions can also be created to specifications. For details, contact the Special Sales Department, Sky Pony Press, 307 West 36th Street, 11th Floor, New York, NY 10018 or info@skyhorsepublishing.com.

Sky Pony® is a registered trademark of Skyhorse Publishing, Inc.®, a Delaware corporation.

Visit our website at www.skyponypress.com.

10 9 8 7 6 5 4 3 2

Library of Congress Cataloguing-in-Publication Data is available on file.

ISBN: 978-1-62914-795-6

Printed in the United States of America

CONTENTS

ACKNOWLEDGMENTS

We would like to thank our great editor, Kelsie Besaw, for her never-ending support, organization, and excitement on these projects. To Sara Kitchen, for working tirelessly on the design and layout until it was perfect. Thank you to Bill Wolfsthal, Tony Lyons, and Linda Biagi for making this project both possible and successful. We would also like to give a big thank-you to everyone at Skyhorse for continuing to do a fantastic job with this series. Extra appreciation goes to Allan Penn, for sticking with us throughout the project, adding more cowbell, and for producing beautiful photography. Thank you to Holly Schmidt for guiding us through this series.

Our warmest regards go to each of our contributors, who provided us with truly remarkable, fun, and creative projects to include in this book: thank you Alexandria Seda; Amber Wylie of Hobo Cat Creations; Kate Schultz of Izzalicious Designs (www.izzalicious.com); DIY Mommy on Youtube; and www.elegantfashion360.com.

Finally, this book would not be the same without the smiling faces of Alden Glovsky, Caleb and Owen Schmidt, and Lily and Fletcher Waterman. Thank you!

Project contributors:
Alexandria Seda: Medusa; Merman; Butterfly; Alien; Penguin; Crab; Baby Mouse
Amber Wylie of Hobo Cat Creations: Cat; Ladybug
Kate Schultz of Izzalicious Designs: Starfish; Dragon; Santa; Superhero; Feisty Fish; Princess; Robot; Garden Gnome
DIY Mommy on Youtube: Pegasus; Parrot
www.elegantfashion360.com: Duck; Dog; Spider; Pig; Bunny; Gingerbread Man

GLOSSARY

Here is a list of some of the terms we use when explaining how to do each project. Getting to know them will help you speed through all these great designs!

hook: The hook is the off-white, hook-shaped utensil that is provided in the packaging of your loom. This is used to move rubber bands from their pegs instead of your fingers.

c-clip: A c-clip, as its name suggests, is a small, clear clip shaped like a "c" that we use to hold rubber bands together. C-clips are often the last step in a project. Some rubber band kits come with s-clips instead; you can use those the same way you use c-clips.

threading: To thread beads onto your project, wrap a thin piece of wire—such as a stripped twist-tie—around a single band. Add the beads onto the wire from the other end, and then slide them onto the band.

Set up your loom square: When all of the columns are evenly set on the loom; no column of pegs is set forward or backward.

offset: When columns in the loom are not square. For example, when the outside columns are set evenly and the middle column is set one peg closer to you.

Making a chain or **"knitting":** To make a chain for arms or feet, wrap a single band around your hook three or four times so it looks like a knot. Attach a double band to the end of the hook, and slide the knot onto this double band. Move everything back onto the shaft of the hook. Continue this process of adding double bands to the chain until you have the desired length.

How to "Loop" your project back: When you have finished putting down all of your rubber bands on the loom, there is one more step before you can remove your project from the loom. This step connects your bands to each other instead of just to the loom.

To Loop Your Project:

1. Start at the peg indicated in the instructions; usually it is the last or second-to-last peg in your project or the peg where you have put a cap band.

2. Use your plastic hook tool and slide it into the hollow space in the middle of the peg to grab the top un-looped band on the peg.

3. Then pull the band up and off the peg, pulling it through any cap bands or any looped bands stacked above it.

4. Attach the band on your hook to the peg where the other end of the same band is still attached. If there is more than one band, loop all the bands on a peg before you move on to loop the next peg.

5. Pegs are typically looped in the opposite order from how you laid them out on the loom, but be sure to follow any specific instructions for the project you are working on.

6. When you have finished looping your project, you should have a few loose loops remaining on the last peg on the loom. You need to secure those loops by tying a band around them or using a c-clip or your project will unravel!

PARROT

This feathered friend is cute and colorful! He's not too tricky; just pay attention to the color changes!

Difficulty level: **Medium**

You need:

1 loom • 1 hook • red, blue, yellow, black, and white bands

To Make the Legs:

1. Lay out your parrot's legs using single bands that have been wrapped once over themselves so they are tight. You can do this by wrapping a band twice around your hook and stretching it over the pegs. To make the feet, wrap a single yellow band around your hook four times and slide it onto a single yellow band that has been wrapped like the leg bands. Repeat three times for each foot.

2. Turn your loom and loop your legs. Secure the ends with a red band and put aside.

To Make the Tail:

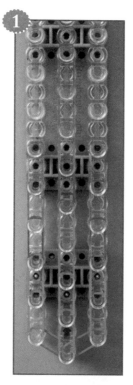
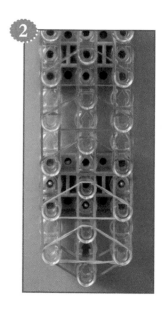

1. Attach double red bands to the first center pegs, and connect them to the right. Repeat and connect them to the left; then repeat one more time and connect to the center. Lay a line of double bands down each column, switching to blue as shown. You will have

a total of two red double bands and three blue double bands lining the outer columns and four red double bands and four blue double bands lining the center column. Wrap a blue cap band around each of the last pegs twice.

2. Wrap a red band around your hook twice and attach it to the first row in a triangle shape. Repeat four more times down the loom.

3. Turn your loom and loop your bands back to where they started. Secure the final loops with double red bands.

To Make the Wings:

1. Attach a single red band to the first middle peg, and connect it to the right. Lay a line of single bands down the middle and right columns, changing color, as shown. Wrap a red "holding" band around the fourth middle peg three times.

2. Wrap a yellow band around your hook twice, then attach it to the second pegs in the right and center columns. Repeat on the next two rows using blue bands. Wrap a blue cap band around the last peg in each row three times.

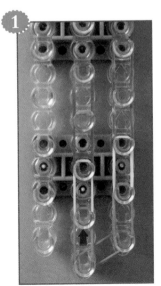

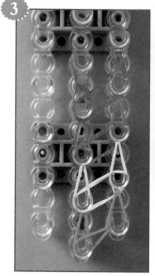

3. Turn your loom and loop your wing. Secure the loose loops and set it aside. Repeat to make your second wing.

To Make the Whole Body:

1. Using red double bands, lay out a hexagon shape onto the loom. Lay down the left side, then the right. Lay out a line of red double bands down the center of the hexagon.

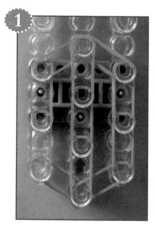

2. Lay a larger hexagon shape onto your loom below the first, using red double bands. For the diagonal bands at the end, take the feet you set aside and untie the double red bands. Place the double bands at the bottom of the hexagon shape. Lay a line of red double bands down the center of the larger hexagon.

3. Place double red bands onto the second and third rows of the larger hexagon in a triangle shape. Take your wings and attach the loose loops to the first outside pegs in the larger hexagon shape, then attach the red "holding" band to the peg just above the feet.

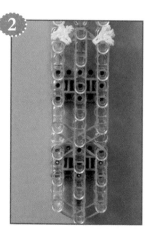

4. To make the eyes, wrap a white band around your hook twice, then wrap a black band around your hook three times. Loop the first white band

around your hook two more times. Repeat to make your second eye. Thread the white and black bands onto a single red band.

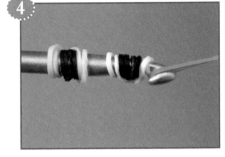

5. Place the eye bands onto the second row of your loom. Wrap a yellow band around your hook four times, then thread them onto two yellow bands doubled over (like you did with the feet). Put both ends of the doubled yellow bands onto the hook, then thread them onto a single red band. Place the beak onto the third row. Place a single red band around the second and third rows in a triangle shape.

6. Place the tail on the last peg on the loom.

7. Turn your loom and loop as usual. Secure the final loose loops with red double bands pulled in a slipknot.

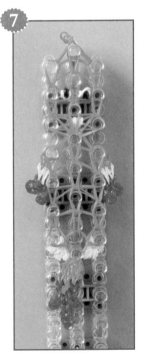

8. Remove your parrot!

BABY MOUSE

Say cheese! This little mouse makes a perfect pet because he doesn't bite or make a mess. Just don't let your cat catch him!

Difficulty level: **Easy**

You need:

1 loom • 1 hook • white, pink, and black bands

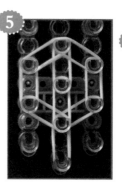

Set up your loom offset, with the middle column pulled one toward you and the arrow facing away.

1. Lay a line of pink bands all the way down your loom. Wrap the bands around the pegs twice; this keeps the bands tight. Wrap a pink cap band around the last peg four times. This is your mouse's tail.

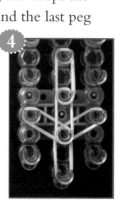

2. Turn your loom and loop your bands back to where they started.

3. Remove your tail from the loom and set it aside.

4. Attach white double bands to the first middle peg, and connect them to the next middle peg. Attach white double bands to the second middle peg, connect them to the right, and then repeat and connect them to the left. Lay a line of double bands from the second middle peg to the fourth.

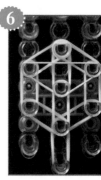

5. Lay out white double bands to finish your hexagon shape. Lay out the left side, then the right side.

6. Wrap a white band around your hook twice, then place it into the third row in a triangle shape.

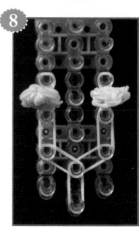

7. Turn your loom around and loop your mouse's ear shape. Remove from the loom and repeat to make a second ear.

8. Attach a double white band to the first middle peg, and connect it to the next middle peg. Begin

laying out a long hexagon shape: lay out the left side, then the right side. Use your hook to thread white double bands through the end loops of your ear shape and attach the bands to the third and fourth pegs in the outside columns.

9. Use double white bands to finish laying out your long hexagon shape. Lay a line of double white bands down the center of your shape.

10. Place the mouse's tail on the last center peg.

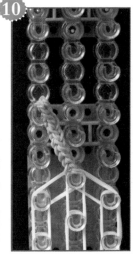

11. Wrap a white band around your hook twice, then place it on the third row in a triangle shape. Wrap two single black bands around your hook three times, then use your hook to thread them onto the triangle band you just placed on the loom.

12. Wrap a white band around your hook twice and place it onto the fourth row on the loom in a triangle shape. Repeat for rows 5 through 7.

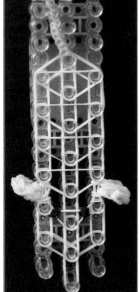

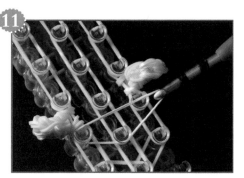

13. Turn your loom around and begin looping your bands back to where they started. When you reach the bands on the ear pegs, pull the ears through the loops before you loop them back onto the peg so that the ears remain standing.

14. Remove your mouse from the loom and thread a double pink band through the last white loops at his nose. Break a white band and use it to tie a knot around the pink bands between the nose and your hook. Cut the end of the pink bands and trim the white tie-off bands, then turn the pink bands so the knot is hidden in his snout.

DRAGON

This friendly dragon may not be a fire-breather, but he sure sets a spark. Although this project has several steps, it is well worth the effort! If you have some time and a couple of looms, you won't find a better pal than this cute little monster.

Difficulty level: **Medium**

You need:

2 looms • 1 hook • 2 black beads • dark green, lime green, and gold bands

Set up two looms connected side by side with the middle column of both looms offset and pulled one peg closer to you.

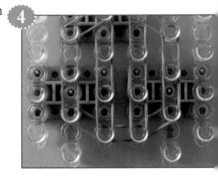

1. Connect the first two middle pegs on your combined loom with double green bands. Attach two green bands to each of the middle pegs, and connect them to the next peg up and away from the center.

2. Attach two more green bands to each middle peg, and connect them to the next peg in the column.

3. Continue laying a line of double green bands up the two middle columns, ending on the fourth peg.

4. Using green double bands, lay out a circle shape for your dragon's head.

5. Using green double bands, lay out the body shape, as shown.

6. Lay double bands down both center columns; use lime green bands for his tummy.

7. Lay out more double bands down the four middle columns to fill in his belly shape.

8. Lay lime green bands down the two center columns, starting where your last green bands left

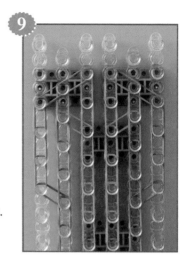

off (the tenth peg) and ending on the second-to-last peg.

9. Lay down a diagonal line of dark green double bands, starting at the outside column where you ended the dark green body bands and ending on the second-to-last middle peg. Do the same on both sides.

To Make the Feet:

1. Wrap three green bands onto your hook three times. Use your hook to "knit" a chain two loops long with the three wrapped bands on the end. (See Glossary for knitting instructions.)

2. Place the four loose loops on your hook onto the second-to-last peg from the end in the middle column. Repeat to make the other foot.

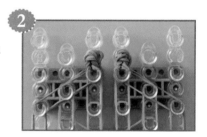

To Make the Ears:

1. Wrap two bands around your hook three times. Use your hook to "knit" a chain one loop long with the two triple-looped bands on the end.

2. Place the loose loops from your hook onto the second peg in the column one in from the outside. Do the same on the other side for the other ear.

To Make the Arms:

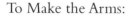

1. Wrap two dark green bands onto your hook three times. Use your hook to "knit" a chain four loops long with the two wrapped bands at the end.

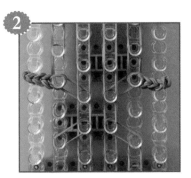

2. Slide all the loose loops from your arm onto the sixth peg, one column in. Repeat to make a second arm, and attach it on the other side.

To Make the Tail:

1. Wrap a dark green band around your hook three times. Use your hook to "knit" a chain eight loops long with the wrapped band at the end.

2. On your last stitch, leave the other end of the two bands off the hook. Stretch a single band between your hook and your finger.

3. Thread the two bands from your hook onto the single band, then slide both ends of the single band onto the hook. Thread the remaining two loops from your tail onto a single band in the same way.

4. Attach your tail to the loom.

Looping Your Dragon:

1. Wrap a cap band twice around the two middle pegs in the fourth, fifth, sixth, and seventh rows.

2. Stretch a single band in a trapezoid shape, as shown, starting at the two middle pegs in the second row, and then repeat in the third row.

3. Lay vertical bands across your dragon's body shape.

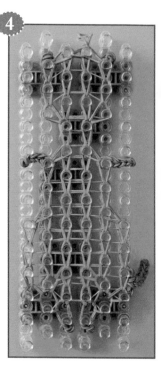

4. Starting at your dragon's feet, begin looping your bands back to where they started.

5. Secure the final loose loops on the loom. Remove your dragon.

To Make the Snout and Eyes:

1. Wrap three dark green bands onto your hook three times. Use your hook to "knit" a chain two loops long with the three bands at the end.

2. Remove your loops from the hook. Pull one end of the loops through the other end and pull it tight.

3. Use your hook to pull the single loop from the snout through the back of the dragon, then pull it through a different loop back to the front. Put the snout through the loop to secure it. Do the same for the other side.

4. Thread a single green band through a black bead. Use your hook to pull the loops from the single band to the back of the dragon's head, and secure them with a c-clip.

To Make the Wings:

1. Set up one loom offset, with the middle column pulled toward you one peg.

2. Attach two gold bands to the first middle peg, and connect them to the next peg to the right. Attach two more gold bands, and connect them to the left. Then attach two more gold bands to the center peg, and connect them to the next middle peg.

3. Lay a line of gold double bands down each column, ending on the fifth peg in the left and middle columns and the fourth peg in the right column.

4. Wrap a single gold band around the pegs in the second row twice to make a triangle shape. Continue laying triangle shapes down your wing shape, as shown.

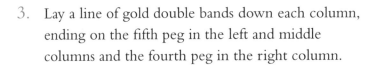

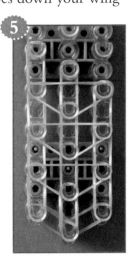

5. Wrap a single cap band twice around each of the last pegs in your three columns.

6. Turn your loom around. Loop all of the bands back to the first middle peg. Loop two green bands through the loops on the last peg, and pull it tight.

7. Remove your wing from the loom.

8. Stick your hook through the front of your dragon, and pull the two green bands from your wing though.

9. Put your hook through the back of the dragon and pull the bands back through another loop. Pull the wing through the bands to secure it.

10. Repeat to make and attach the other wing.

SANTA

Santa is coming to your loom! This jolly figure is great for Christmas or any time of year. Be prepared to show off your best loom skills, because this project takes a lot of time and concentration! You will need an extended loom, meaning two looms attached vertically. You will also need two extra columns on either side of the top loom for his big belly. We know this is a lot, so if you only have one loom, consider sharing looms with friends and working on this project as a team. Merry looming!

Difficulty level: **Hard**

You need:

2 looms + 2 columns • 1 regular hook • 1 fine hook • 1 c-clip • red, white, pink, and black bands • 1 gold band

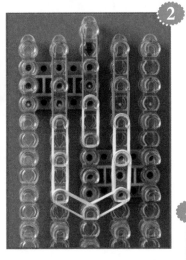

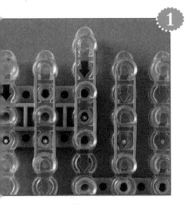

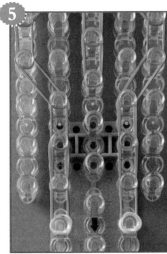

Set up a loom with the center column offset one peg away from you. All of the bands will be double bands except for the neck.

1. For each of the middle three columns, attach two rows of red double bands to make his hat, as shown.

2. To make his head, you will use white double bands for his white hair, laying them out, as shown.

3. Add two sets of double bands inside his face. We used pink bands for this Santa's face, but you can use whatever color you like.

4. Attach a white triple band for his neck. Just below, use red double bands for the shoulders and belly.

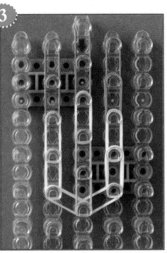

5. For Santa's legs, add three more sets of red double bands for both the second and

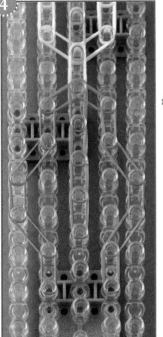

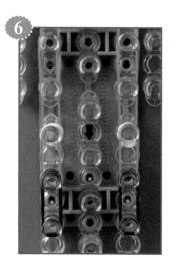

third columns. For the white fluffy cuff, triple-loop two single white bands and place each on the pegs in the second and third column.

6. Attach red double bands to the second and third columns, and then a set of black triple bands for each boot.

7. For the sole of his boot, take a black triple band and wrap it around your hook three times like a knot. Then take two bands and attach one end to the hook.

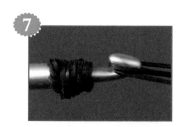

8. Slide the knot down the hook and over the bands.

9. Fold the bands and connect them to the pegs at the bottom of his legs for the boots.

10. Fill in his belly with red double bands, as shown.

11. For his arms, take a black triple band and wrap them around your hook three times. Attach a white double band to the

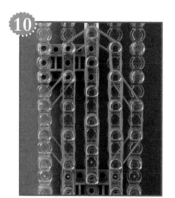

hook, and slide the knot down over the white band. Slide this up the hook, and then attach a red band to the hook.

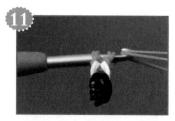

12. Slide the white and black knot over the red double bands. Repeat this twice to create his arm.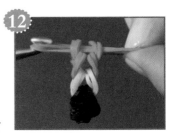

13. Attach his arms to the loom at the shoulders. To secure the figure, you will place a series of triangular crossover bands. Do this as seen in the photo, for a total of seven crossover bands.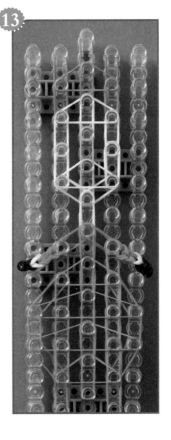

14. Thread two black beads over a white band to create the eyes and attach to his face.

Looping:

1. Begin with Santa's boots. Do not loop the white "puffs" at his feet; hold the white bands 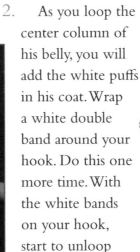 while you loop the red. Loop all the bands in the belly except the center column, starting with the outside columns.

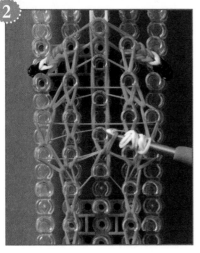

2. As you loop the center column of his belly, you will add the white puffs in his coat. Wrap a white double band around your hook. Do this one more time. With the white bands on your hook, start to unloop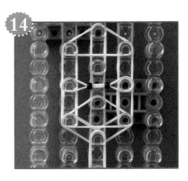

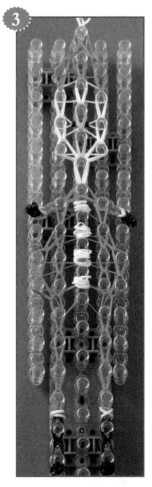

the next red band in the center column. Before you loop it back to the peg where it started, slide the white bands down onto the red band, and then secure it on the peg. Repeat this to the top of his suit or for a total of four puffs.

3. Loop the rest of the project until the top red bands. Pull the two red outside bands to the top center peg to create the peak of his hat. Using your hook, knot a white double band at the very last peg.

4. Remove the project from the loom very carefully.

To Make the Belt and Beard:

1. Wrap two black bands around his belly. Take a single gold band and hook it through his belt.

2. Pull the gold band through the body to his back and secure with a c-clip. Repeat this process for his buttons, but using single black bands up the white of his coat.

3. Take a single white band and feed it from the back of his head to the front of his face for half a mustache.

4. Keeping it on the hook, feed it through one of the white bands in side of his head. Take

another single white band and attach it to the end of the hook, as shown.

5. Pull this band through the bands in his face.

6. Knot the band on itself. Extend the band by feeding a new band through it and knotting it in the same way.

7. Loop another single band over your hook three times. Do this until your band is full, and attach to the band on Santa's face.

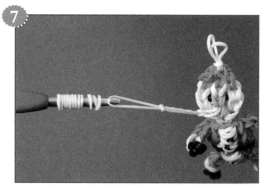

8. Slide the loops down onto the band from the hook to form the beard. Like you did with the first part of the mustache, feed another white band through his face, knot it, and feed it through a white band in the side of his face. Attach the beard, adding extension bands if necessary.

9. Using the extension bands, repeat the same process as the beard to create the puff in his hat. To secure, feed the end of the puff through the side of his head. Secure this band to the c-clip in the back of his

body, threading through other bands if necessary so the body doesn't bend.

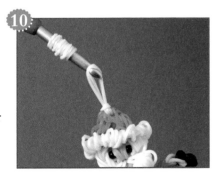

10. To make the pompom in his hat, wrap a band three times around your hook; repeat twice. Grab the white loop at the top of Santa's hat with this hook.

11. Slide these bands onto the loop. Feed your hook through the base of Santa's hat and grab the top of the white loop.

12. Pull the loop back through the base of Santa's hat.

13. Then wrap the loop over the top of the pompom to secure it.

SUPERHERO

What's that flying through the air? It's your own superhero, here to make your day! Swap out the colors to make him however you'd like. You can even make a whole team to help him fight crime! If you have only one loom, you can still make this project: just make the arms first, then loop and remove them from the loom. Before you loop your superhero, place the arms onto the shoulders. His shoulders won't be as wide and muscular when you build him this way.

Difficulty level: **Medium**

You need:

1 loom • 1 hook • 1 c-clip • black, blue, red, peach, and white bands • 1 clear band

Set up your loom with five columns, offset: pull the outside and center columns one peg closer to you.

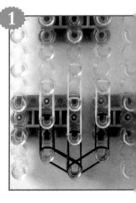

To Make Your Hero:

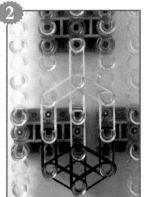

1. Attach black double bands to the first middle peg, and connect them to the left. Repeat and connect them to the right. Attach another pair of black bands, and attach them to the next middle peg. Lay double bands down the three middle columns, as shown, starting with black bands, then using different bands for your superhero's face, in this case peach.

2. Place diagonal black double bands from the first outside pegs to the second middle peg to finish off his hair. Place diagonal peach double bands from the third outside pegs to the fourth center peg. Connect three bands to the fourth middle peg, and connect them to the next middle peg.

3. Lay diagonal lines of blue triple bands from the neck to the sixth outside peg on both sides. Lay a line of blue double bands down the center column, ending on the fourth peg from the end.

4. Lay a line of blue double bands down the columns on either side of the center. Use red bands for the last two sets of bands.

5. Wrap three red bands around your hook three times, then thread

them through three red
bands. Put all the loops
from the last red bands
on your hook, then put it
onto the red "boot" band
at the end of the loom.
Repeat, and place the
other foot on the other
red boot.

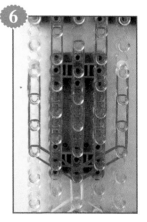

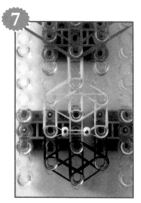

6. Lay double blue bands
    down the outside
    columns for the arms.
    Wrap two peach
    bands around your
    hook three times, then
    thread them through
    another two peach
    bands. Place the hands
    onto the pegs at the
    end of the arms, as
    you did with the feet.

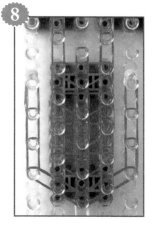

7. Thread two white beads onto a single peach
    band, then attach it to the second row. Use a
    marker to draw on his pupils. Place a single peach
    band onto the third row in a triangle shape.

8. Place a single blue band across the sixth row
    (just below his shoulders) in a triangle shape. Wrap a blue band
    around your hook twice, and attach it to the seventh row in a triangle
    shape. Do the same across the next two rows.

9. Turn your loom around and loop your bands back to where they
    started. Make sure that where you laid out three bands you are also

looping back three bands. Secure the final loose loops with a clear band pulled through itself like a slipknot.

10. Remove your superhero from the loom and set him aside.

To Make the Cape:

1. Lay a diagonal line of red double bands from the first center peg to the second outside peg, first laying out the left side, then doing the same on the right.

2. Lay a line of red double bands down each column on your loom, ending on the seventh peg for the three center columns and the eighth peg for the outside columns.

3. Lay a single red band across each row, as shown.

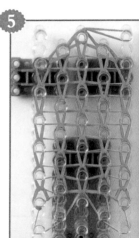

4. Pull the horizontal bands at the bottom up and past the last middle peg.

5. Turn your loom around and loop your bands back to where they started. Secure the final loose loops with a double red band, and remove your cape from the loom.

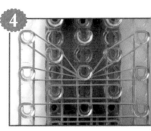

6. Use your hook to pull single bands through your superhero to make his mouth and a chest emblem. Secure the bands to a single c-clip on his back.

7. Slide the loops from his cape over his neck to finish your superhero!

FeiSTY FiSH

Whether you love goldfish, the rowdy beta, or fascinating tropical navigators, this fish will go right along with any school in your loom collection! The body of the fish is simple to make, but the fins can get a little tricky, as you will be looping bands almost as if you are knitting. Once you have this down, you will have your fish friend in no time!

Difficulty level: **Easy**

You need:

1 loom • 2 hooks • 2 beads • 1 threader • rubber bands of different colors

Set up your loom horizontally and so that the center column is offset by one peg. You will use two different colors to create double bands. All bands are double, unless otherwise mentioned.

1. Using your double bands, lay out the figure shown. The white band is a triple band and will be where the eyes go.

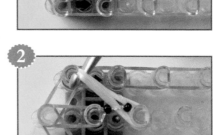

2. Thread a clear single band through two black beads for the eyes. Unhook one side of the white triple band from the loom, and place one side of the clear single band down. Replace the white bands, weave the clear single band through its center, and secure it to the loom.

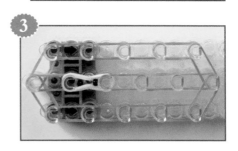

3. Lay out the rest of the fish body, as shown.

4. To make the fins, you will create a bundle of knots. First, wrap a single band around your hook and slide it onto another single band.

5. Wrap another knot on your hook, and slide it onto the bundle you just made, reattaching the bundle to your hook afterward.

6. Wrap a band on itself once. Slide the bundle of bands onto this band.

7. Slide this bundle onto another single band, knotting it.

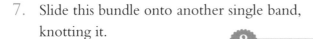

8. Repeat this process to make a second fin. Unhook one of the double bands from the loom, and attach the first fin.

9. Replace the double band that you moved over the first fin. Attach the second fin.

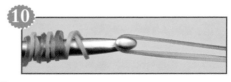

10. Wrap single bands once onto your hook, alternating colors and repeating until the hook is full. Slide these onto a double band and then reattach to the hook.

11. Slide this bundle onto another double band, and stretch the band across the pegs at the top of the fish's body.

12. For the big fin, wrap a double band around your hook and slide it onto another double band until you have two bundles. Slide one side of one of these bundles onto another double band, switching up your colors if you like.

13. Move this new bundle back onto your hook.

14. Repeat this process to make several bundles, keeping them all connected.

15. Slide the entire bundle onto a new double band, knotting this one so that you have a full fin.

16. Place the big fin at the end of the fish's body on the loom.

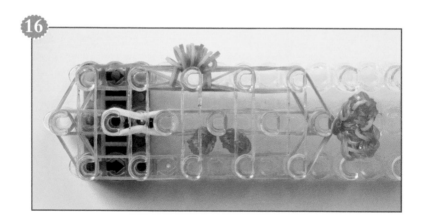

17. Loop the bands back to the pegs where they started, beginning with the tail of the fish and working left. Tie off the project with a band before removing it from the loom.

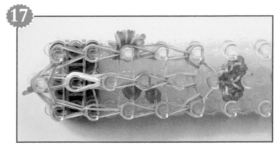

PRINCeSS

Celebrate your loom fun with these beautiful fairy princesses! This project requires one loom and two additional columns for the princess' hair and dresses. If you only have one loom, you can make some of these parts off the loom and then connect them before you loop. You could also pool looms with a friend and make matching princesses together!

Set up your loom with the arrows facing toward you and the center column offset away from you. Attach one column on either side of the loom. All bands are double bands unless otherwise mentioned.

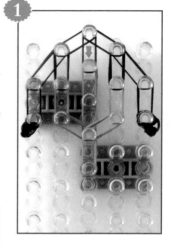

1. Lay out double bands for the hair and face. The band for her neck should be a triple band. Knit a short chain (one knot slid over two sets of double bands) for each of her pigtails, and attach to the ends of her hair.

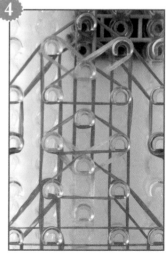

2. Lay out the princess's body, as shown. You will need to switch between colors for her skin, her dress, and the accent on her dress. Like her pigtails, make very short chains to add for her hands and feet.

3. Lay out single crossover bands across her dress. The band at the bottom should tuck behind the last center peg.

4. For her torso, lay out three single triangle crossover bands that have been wrapped once on themselves so they are taut.

5. Thread beads over a band for her eyes and attach to her face. Attach a single triangle crossover band over her face. Then, stretch two crossover bands wide across her face.

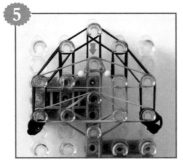

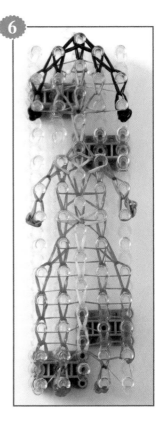

6. Starting from her shoes, loop the project back all the way up to the top. When looping the skirt and the arms, loop the outside first and work your way in. Make sure to remember to loop the accent in the middle of her dress, as well as the accent at her shoulders. Secure the project with a rubber band at the top.

7. Carefully remove the princess from the loom. Thread a pink band through her face for her lips and secure it behind her head. Form a short chain with gold bands and thread that through her hair to make a tiara, securing it at the back of her head as well. Use a marker to draw pupils in her eyes.

ROBOT

R2-who? Like no robot you've ever seen, this amazing bionic cyclops will be the coolest addition to your loom fun! Attach him to your backpack, glue him to a refrigerator magnet, or line him up with a whole army of robots! Our robot is silver, but the step-by-step photos are shown in bright green for better viewing. Metallic bands tend to be very thick, so be careful throughout your looming process to prevent them from snapping. While these instructions show how to create the robot in one loom with two columns, it is no problem if you only have one loom! The extra columns are for the arms, which can be done separately and then added to the figure. Now get in touch with your cyborg side and get cracking on this awesome project!

Difficulty level: **Medium**

You need:

1 loom **or** 1 loom + 2 columns • 1 regular hook • 1 fine hook • 6 beads • 1 googly eye • 1 flat-top button • silver and white bands

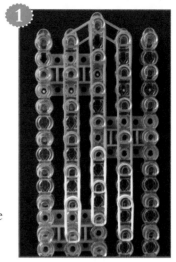

Set the loom up so that the arrows are pointing toward you. The center column should be offset by one peg moved away from you. All the bands will be double bands.

1. Using silver and white bands, lay out the shape, as shown. Use silver bands where we've put the green bands.

2. Continue laying your line of double bands down the columns next to the center, switching back to silver bands. These are his legs.

3. For his feet, create a triple band and wrap it around your hook twice so it looks like a knot. Take another triple band, and attach to the end of your hook, as shown.

4. Slide the knotted bands onto the center of the triple band, like in the photo.

5. Wrap it around the very bottom left peg in the loom to make his foot. Repeat this again for his right foot.

6. To make the body sturdier, you will create three triangles out of single silver bands called crossover bands. Starting

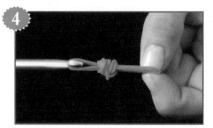

from the very bottom peg in the center column (where the body ends and the legs begin), wrap a crossover band around this peg and the two pegs below it on the left and right, so it looks like a triangle. Going up the body, make two more triangles, like in the photo.

7. For his computer, slide three beads onto your fine hook. Attach a white single band to the end of your hook, and slide the beads over the band. Stretch the band a little and attach it across the white pegs in the middle of his body. Do this with two beads for the row above, as shown. If your beads do not fit over the hook, see the section in our glossary on bead threading.

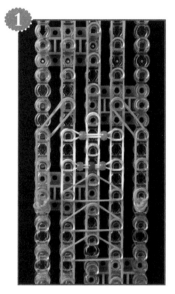

To Make the Arms:

If you have just one loom, you will need to make the arms separately and then attach them to the fourth pegs in the left and right columns. The following photos show the project using extra columns.

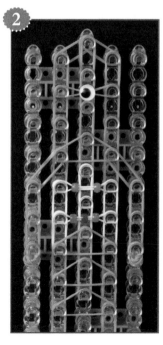

1. Attach silver double bands diagonally to the outside columns from his shoulders (the fourth pegs on the right and left columns), and then create the arms like in the photo. To make the hands, repeat steps 3 through 5 with double bands instead of triple, and attach them to the bottom of his arms.

2. Attach a single crossover band at the shoulders to connect the arms. For the eye, use a googly eye bead or a bead with a flat face and glue a googly eye to the bead.

Thread a single silver band through the eye, and attach it to the face, as shown.

Looping:

1. Start with the feet. Hold the feet down so they do not come unattached from the pegs, and loop the bands back to the pegs where they originated. Do the legs first, then the body, and then the arms and head. When you reach the first crossover band at the top of his legs, tuck this band up behind the center peg. You will loop this with the bands on the bottom peg in the center column. At the top of the robot's head, tie a band through the top band and pull it tight to knot it.

2. Gently remove the project from the loom.

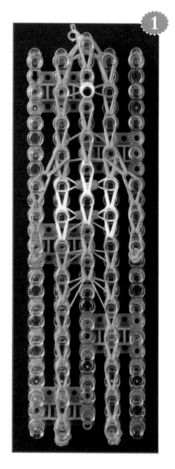

To Make the Mask:

1. Knit a single chain or fishtail stitch in white bands.

2. Wrap the mask over the robot's face, making sure to snugly secure the bands around the googly eye. Secure the mask behind the robot's head with an s- or c-clip.

GARDEN GNOME

Whether he hides in your garden or hangs off your backpack, this garden gnome is awesome. This project requires an extended loom because his body is wide. If you do not have access to extra columns, you can make the sides of his body off the loom, loop them, and then attach the sides to the regular loom before you loop the rest of the body back. (To see this process in action, please refer to the Medusa project on page 89.) Now get gnoming!

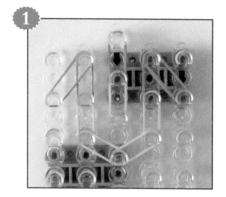

Set up your loom so the center column is offset one peg away from you. Attach one column on either side of the loom. All bands are double bands unless otherwise mentioned.

1. Lay out red and orange double bands for the first part of his head, as shown.

2. Continue by laying out white double bands for his beard.

3. Start his torso with black and green double bands.

4. Make his pants with gray double bands.

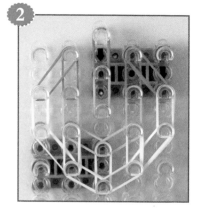

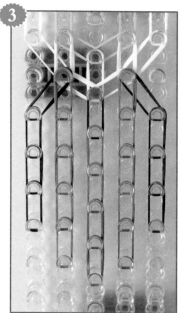

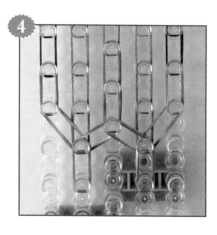

5. Attach black triple bands for his feet. Wrap a black double band around your hook and slide it onto another black triple band and attach it to the loom for the sole of his shoe.

6. Using orange and black double bands, knit two chains for his arms and attach them to the loom at his shoulders. Stretch four single gray crossover bands over his torso.

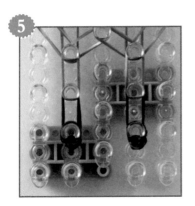

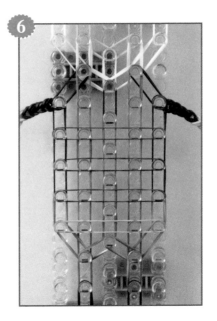

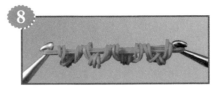

7. Attach an orange crossover band to the gnome's face, and add eyes by threading a single clear band through two black beads.

8. Create four separate knots by wrapping a red double band around your hook and sliding it over another red double band. Slide all of these onto one red double band, and knot it together to make a bouquet.

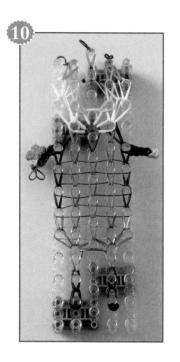

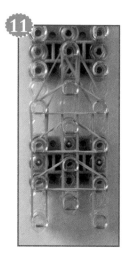

9. Wrap it with a green double band and pull it through the gnome's hand.

10. Loop the bands back very carefully. When doing the torso, loop the outside columns first (including the shoulders), then the inside. Secure the red bands at the top. This will be temporary while you make his hat.

11. Using a regular loom with the center column offset, build his hat with red double bands. Attach single crossover bands to the loom; these should be wrapped once on themselves so that they are taut.

12. Knit a short chain of red double bands, and attach it to the very top of his hat. Attach his body to the bottom of the hat. Starting

from the bottom of the hat, loop the bands back to the pegs where they started, going all the way up to the pointy part in his hat. Secure with a red double band or a c-clip and remove from the loom.

13. Wrap several single bands individually onto your hook. Slide them onto an extended single band to create the puffs in his beard (several single bands knotted together to make one long band). Attach the beard to his face by threading the ends through his hair and tying

it at the back. To make the beard longer, repeat this process but attach the extension to the bottom of his beard. This will also help secure his beard to the bottom of his face.

CAT

This friendly feline is perfect for your loom menagerie! While the ears can be a little tricky to loop because the bands are tightly wrapped, the rest of this project is super easy to put together. Play a game of cat and mouse with the other creatures in this book, or let this kitten purr on its own!

To Make the Ears:

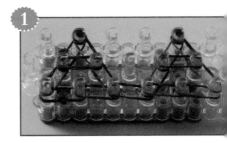

1. Set up your loom horizontally, with the center column offset toward the left. Using single black bands that have been wrapped once on themselves, lay out two triangles that are connected by a band in between. Add a triple-wrapped crossover band to each triangle. Add a cap band that has been wrapped five times to both top points of the triangles.

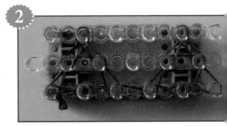

2. Loop back by starting from the points and working down. Loop the long bottom row of bands last, starting from the far right and moving to the far left. Before removing from the loom, tie a double-wrapped single band (in a slipknot) to both ends of the project to secure it. You will need these when you attach the ears to the body.

To Make the Body:

1. Now, set up your loom vertically with the arrows facing toward you (and the center column still offset). Lay out the body of the cat using all double bands, except for the neck, where it will be a triple band. The white feet at the bottom should have cap bands that have been wrapped three times.

2. Make a long single chain with about six black double bands for the tail.

Make two shorter single chains—starting with white double bands and then switching to black—for the front legs. Attach the tail, legs, and ears to the loom where shown.

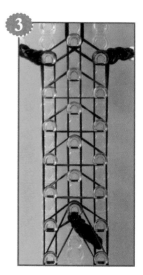

3. Lay out four triangle crossover bands over the cat's belly. The bottom one should be wrapped once on itself so that it is tighter. Then, attach a band diagonally on either side of the tail and another two bands stretched diagonally to just below the tail.

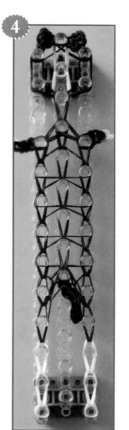

4. Starting from the feet, loop the bands back up until you reach the chin. Do not loop any farther than this just yet.

5. Make the muzzle on your cat's face by attaching white double bands in a diamond shape. Then, slide a wrapped pink single band over a white single band, and stretch it across the muzzle.

6. Starting from the bottom of the muzzle, carefully loop the bands back. Save the top white band for last, and then tie the project off at the top.

7. Carefully pull the cat off the loom. Using your hook, pull four black rubber bands through the pink nose, and then snip the ends of the black bands to make the cat's whiskers. To make the cat stand upright, pull his front paws through a band or two on the edges of his torso.

LADYBUG

Did you know ladybugs are also called ladybirds? What do you call these little beetles? Ladybugs are happiest in a garden, so why not make some flowers to keep her company!

Difficulty level: **Easy**

You need:

1 loom • 1 hook • red and black bands

Set up your loom offset, with the middle column pulled one closer to you and the arrow pointing away.

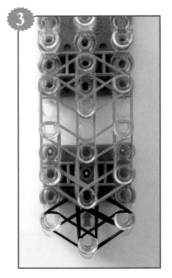

1. Attach two black bands to the first middle peg, and connect them to the next middle peg. Attach another pair of black bands to the first middle peg, and connect them to the peg to the right. Attach another pair of black bands, and connect them to the next peg to the left.

2. Lay a line of double red bands down the middle column, ending on the fifth peg.

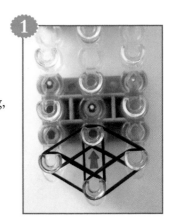

3. Lay a hexagon shape onto the loom using double red bands. Lay out the left side and then the right.

4. Attach two red bands to the third middle peg, then connect them to the next peg to the right. Attach another pair of bands and connect them to the next peg on the left. Do the same with the fourth middle peg.

5. Wrap a black band around your hook three times, and thread it onto a single red band. Repeat to make five total "spots" for your ladybug.

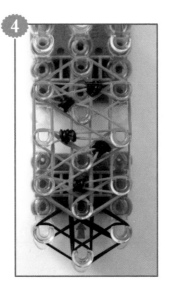

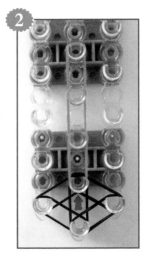

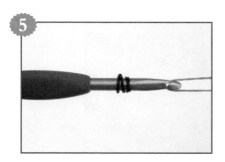

6. Place the bands from your spots onto the loom, as shown.

7. Turn your loom, and begin looping your bands back to where they started. Loop any red diagonal bands back to the center. Loop the first set of black diagonal bands from the center out, and loop the second set of black diagonal bands in to the center.

8. Pull a black band through the loose loops on the last peg, and pull one end of the band through the other like a slipknot.

9. Remove your ladybug from the loom. Knot your finishing loop again, then cut it at the end, and tie a knot at the end of each strand to make the antenna.

PEGASUS

Fly away with this amazing project! This delightful stallion has the best of both fantasy steeds: a sparkly horn like a unicorn and powerful wings like the ancient mythological Pegasus. Your Pegasus will require a few intricate steps, but the outcome is absolutely adorable!

To Make the Legs:

1. Starting on the eighth peg from the end, lay a line of four sets of double pink bands down the left column. Wrap a white band around your hook twice, and attach it to the next two pegs. Repeat to lay doubled white bands down the rest of the column. Wrap a black cap band around the last peg three times, then repeat with a second cap band.

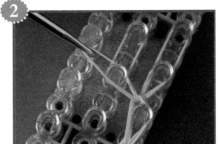

2. To finish the front legs, loop your bands back to where they started and remove your leg from the loom. For the back legs, attach double pink bands to the sixth and seventh pegs from the end in the middle column.

3. Loop your leg as usual until you reach the second to last pink peg. Instead of looping this band back to where it started, loop it to the sixth peg from the end in the middle column.

4. Continue looping your back leg and remove it from the loom. Make two front legs and two back legs.

To Make the Wings:

1. Lay single sparkly bands down the center column, ending on the third peg. Lay out a half hexagon shape on the left side using single sparkly bands, ending on the third middle peg.

2. Lay a line of single sparkly bands up the right column, ending on the fifth peg.

3. Attach a single band to the third middle peg, and connect it to the next middle peg. Attach a single sparkly band to the fourth middle peg, and connect it to the fifth peg on the right. Wrap a cap band around the fifth peg in the right column.

4. Wrap a sparkly band around your hook twice, and place it on the second row in a triangle shape. Wrap another band around your hook twice, and place it on the right and middle columns, as shown.

5. Turn your loom around and loop your wing. Place the loose loops from the final two pegs on your hook and thread them onto two sparkly bands. Repeat to make a second wing.

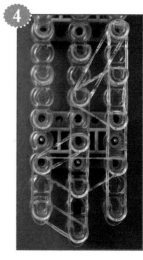

To Make the Whole Body:

1. Use pink double bands to lay a hexagon shape onto the loom. Lay down the right side, then the left.

2. Stack white bands on the first middle peg (we used about ten). Attach two white bands to the first middle peg, and connect them to the next middle peg. Push the white bands onto this band. Repeat with the next peg, using pink double bands between the second and third peg.

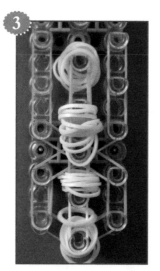

3. Attach a single pink band to the third middle peg, and connect it to the left.

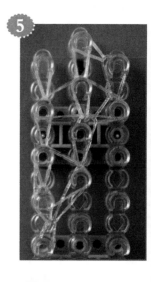

Repeat on the right. Lay a line of single pink bands down the outside columns, ending on the fifth peg. Stack white bands on the fourth middle peg as you did before. Attach three pink bands to the third middle peg, and connect it to the next middle peg. Move the white bands onto the three pink bands. Repeat on the next peg.

4. Starting at the fifth middle peg, use pink double bands to lay out a long hexagon shape. Lay a line of pink double bands down the center of the hexagon.

5. Put all the end loops from your wings onto your hook, then thread them onto a single pink band. Place the pink band onto the second row of your hexagon, in a triangle shape. Tuck the wings down into the loom.

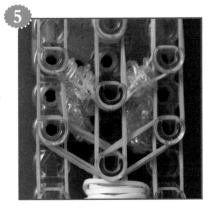

6. Wrap a pink band around your hook three times, then thread it onto pink double bands. Put both ends of the pink double bands on your hook, then put the loops onto the first peg on the left. Repeat, and place the other loop on the right.

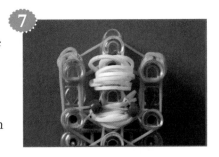

7. Thread two beads onto a single pink band, and attach it to the second row on the loom, in a triangle shape.

8. Place your back legs on the last two pegs in the outside columns.

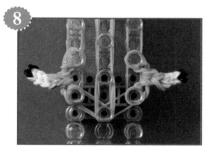

9. Place a single pink band around the pegs in the second row in a triangle shape. Wrap a pink band around the third row two times (or three times, if you can stretch it enough). Wrap a pink band around your hook twice, then attach it to the fourth row in a triangle shape. Place double pink bands across the seventh and eighth rows in a triangle shape.

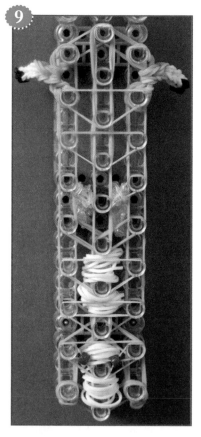

10. Wrap a gold sparkly band around your hook three times. Thread it onto gold sparkly double bands. Use your hook to "knit" a chain four loops long with the wrapped band at the end. Thread the last gold loops through a single pink band and place it on the first row.

11. Turn your loom around and begin looping the outside columns. When you reach the diagonal bands in the fifth row (right after the wings), thread

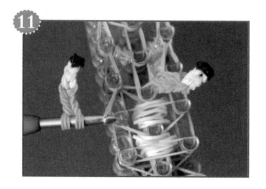

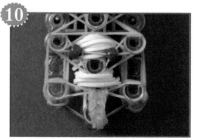

one of the front legs onto your hook, then thread it onto the diagonal band before you loop it back to the middle peg. Do the same on the other side with the other leg.

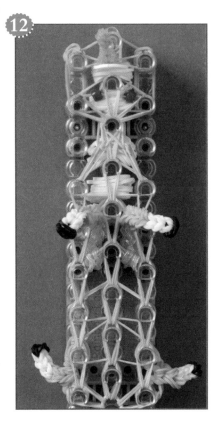

12. Loop the middle pegs, then continue looping the rest of the pegs, ending at the third peg from the end.

13. Lay a line of pink double bands down the center column from the second peg to the fourth. Attach double pink bands to the second peg from the end in the outside columns, and connect them to the third peg. Wrap a pink band around your hook twice. Attach it to the third peg from the end in the outside column, and connect it to the next middle peg. Do the same on the other side.

14. Wrap a pink band around your hook twice, and place it across the second row in a triangle shape. Wrap a pink band around your hook three times, and attach it to the third row. Wrap a pink cap band around the fourth middle peg three times.

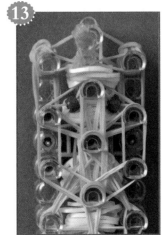

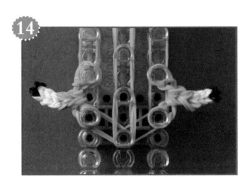

15. Starting at the fourth middle peg, begin looping your Pegasus's face. Before you loop the last three pegs at the top, add a bundle of single white bands to the top center peg; this will be the top of Pegasus's mane. Loop the rest of the bands back as normal to secure the mane. Tie off the project at the top with a rubber band before you remove it from the loom.

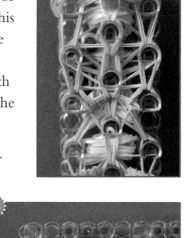

16. To add Pegasus's ponytail, slide a bundle of white single bands over another single band and attach it to the loom. Do this two more times so they are all connected.

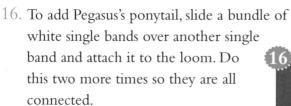

17. Loop the tail back (you do not need a cap band). Remove it from the loom.

Attach the tail to the end of the project by weaving the loose bands through a pink band and tying everything off with a slipknot. You can wrap the loop of the slipknot over the tail to secure.

DUCK

Make your own rubberband duckie! This project is perfect for a rainy day inside or any time you want a happy little yellow bird to brighten your day. Or you can make a whole flock in a rainbow of colors!

Difficulty level: **Easy**

You need:

1 loom • 1 hook • 1 c-clip • yellow and orange bands • 2 black bands

Set up your loom offset, with the middle pegs pulled one peg closer to you.

To Make the Wings and Tail Feathers:

1. Lay a line of double bands down a column, ending on the fourth peg for the wings, as shown, and the third peg for the tail feather pieces. Triple-loop a yellow cap band around the last peg in your line.

2. Turn your loom around. Starting with the peg with the cap band, begin looping your bands back to the peg where they started.

3. Carefully remove your chain from the loom and set aside.

4. Repeat to make two wings and two tail feather pieces.

To Make the Beak:

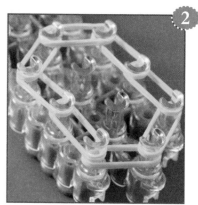

1. Wrap an orange band onto your hook three times. Use your hook to "knit" a chain *two* loops long (one orange, one yellow) with the orange band on the end.

2. Set your beak aside.

To Make the Head and Body:

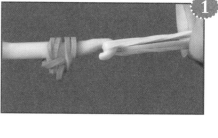

1. Attach two yellow bands to the first middle peg, and connect them to the first peg on the left.

2. Lay out a long hexagon shape onto the loom, as shown. Lay out the left side, then the right side of the shape.

3. Pick up your beak. Attach one end of the yellow band to the third peg on the left and the other end to the third peg on the right.

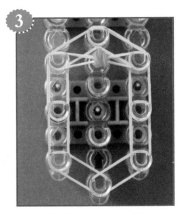

4. Lay a line of double bands down the center of your hexagon.

5. To make the eyes, wrap two black bands separately around your hook three times. Thread them both onto a single yellow band.

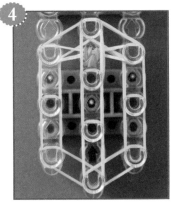

6. Attach the yellow band with your bird's eyes to the second peg on the right and left. Use your hook to pull the middle of the yellow band down to attach it to the second middle peg. Make sure the black "eye" bands are on either side of the middle peg.

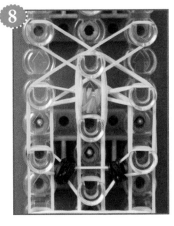

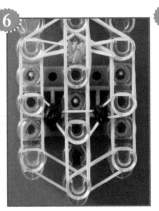

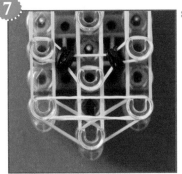

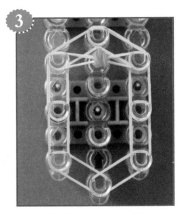

7. Wrap a single band around the bottom right and left pegs twice, as a cap band.

8. Attach a single yellow band to the fourth middle peg, and connect it to the next peg to the left. Attach another single yellow band to the middle peg, and connect it to the right.

9. Lay a long hexagon shape onto the loom, as you did with the head shape. Lay the left side of the shape first, then the right side.

10. Lay out a line of double bands down the center column of your long hexagon shape.

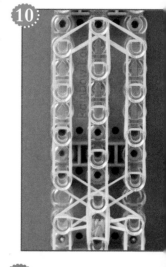

Putting It Together:

1. Take one of the wings, remove the c-clip, and use your hook to slide all four loops onto the fourth peg on the left.

2. Do the same for the other wing, attaching it to the fourth peg on the right.

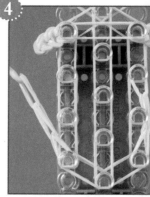

3. Attach two yellow bands to the fourth peg on the right, and connect the other end to the fourth peg on the left (where you attached the wings).

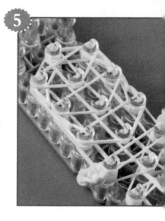

4. Attach the tail feather pieces to your bird: Remove the c-clip and slide all four loops onto the last peg on the left. Grab the other end of the tail feather chain and attach the loop at the end to the fifth peg on the left. Do the same on the right side.

5. Attach two yellow bands to the fifth middle peg and the fifth pegs on the right and left to make a triangle shape. Repeat for the sixth and

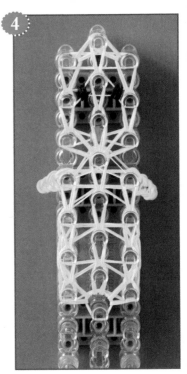

seventh rows, making a triangle shape for each. Wrap a cap band three times onto the last middle peg in your shape.

Looping:

1. Turn your loom around, and starting with the middle peg closest to you, begin looping your bands back onto the pegs where they started.

2. Loop the pegs along the left side of your body shape, then the right. Then, loop the middle bands of the body shape, ending at the middle "neck" peg.

3. From the fifth middle peg (the "neck"), loop all the bands off that peg, first to the middle, then to the left, then to the right. Continue looping the head circle shape as you did the body, first looping the left outside pegs, then the right, then the middle column.

4. Secure the loose loops on the final peg with a single band or with a c-clip, then carefully remove your bird from the loom.

To Add the Feet:

1. Wrap an orange band around your hook four times. Stretch another orange band between the hook and your finger.

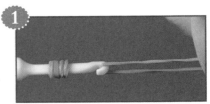

2. Thread the looped band onto the stretched orange band. Pull one end of the single band through the other and pull it snug.

3. Put your hook though the back of your bird, through the four loops at the bottom corner, and grab the remaining loop from your bird's foot. Pull the loop through, then pull the foot through the loop to secure it.

4. Repeat to make the second foot.

DOG

Whe hat a good dog! This little Fido can sit and stay where you put him, and he can even roll over (with a little bit of help)! Make him your best friend, or craft a whole pack to keep him company!

Difficulty level: **Easy**

You need:

1 loom • 1 hook • 1 c-clip • white, black, and red bands

Set up your loom with the pegs square and the arrow pointing away from you.

To Make the Snout:

1. Lay single bands across the first row, moving from left to right. Lay two sets of double bands up the right and left columns, then one pair down the middle.

2. Wrap a black band onto your hook three times. Use your hook to thread it onto two black bands. Attach one end of the double black bands to the second middle peg and the other end to the third middle peg. This is your dog's nose.

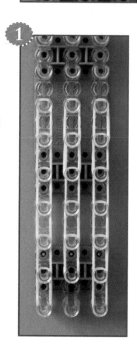

3. Attach two white bands across the second row. Do the same on the third row. Pull the middle of the bands across the third row off the middle peg.

4. Turn your loom around. Loop the pegs along the left side, then the right, and then the middle column.

5. Secure the loose loops from the final peg with a single band and remove the snout from the loom.

To Make the Face:

1. Lay out a line of white double bands up all three columns, ending on the seventh peg. Skip the first peg in the middle column.

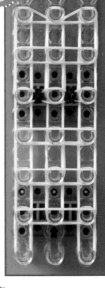

2. Wrap two black bands separately onto your hook three times. Thread the two black bands onto a single white band. Attach the white band for your dog's eyes to the fifth row. Make sure the black bands are separated.

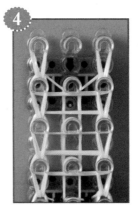

3. Lay white double bands across the second, third, and fourth rows. Skip the fifth row with your dog's eyes, then lay double bands across the sixth and seventh rows in the same way. Pull the bands in the last row toward you, as shown.

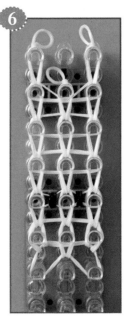

4. Turn your loom around. Loop the pegs on the left side of the loom, then loop the right side. Use your hook to pull the middle of the bands across what is now the second-to-last row toward you, as shown.

5. Loop the middle column.

6. Secure the loose loops on each of the three last pegs with a single band. Remove your dog's face from the loom.

To Add the Snout:

1. Use your hook to pull a white band halfway through your snout, in the same center loop where the black band runs through.

2. Pull both ends of the white band through to the back of the dog's face, and secure the ends with a c-clip.

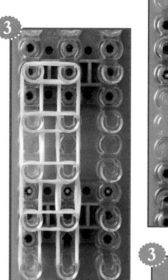

To Make the Legs:

1. Attach a single band to the first two pegs in each the left and middle columns.

2. Lay out a line of white bands down the left and middle columns, ending on the fifth peg. Use single bands to connect rows 1 and 2 and double bands for the rest.

3. Wrap a white cap band twice around the middle and left pegs in rows 2 through 5. You can add an additional double-looped band on the fifth row to make your dog stand better.

4. Turn your loom around and loop your bands back to where they started. Do not loop the horizontal bands.

5. Remove from the loom. Repeat three more times to make your dog's four legs.

To Make the Body:

1. Attach a band to the fifth peg on the left, then connect it to the next peg up and the next peg to the right to make a triangle.

2. Thread the loops from one of your dog legs onto two white bands, and attach the bands to the left column above the triangle. Do the same on the right.

3. Lay a line of double white bands down the rest of the middle column and to the second-to-last peg on the left. Place your third dog leg onto the last two pegs on the left as you did before.

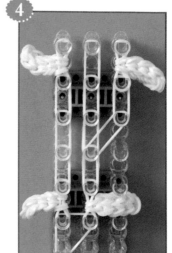

4. Attach a single band to the middle peg four from the end and connect it to the right column. Attach two bands to the peg where you ended your diagonal band, and connect it to the next peg in the right column. Attach your last dog leg to the final two pegs in the right column, as you did before.

5. Lay two white bands across the pegs in the last row. Do the same on the second-to-last row on the loom. Wrap a single band two times across the pegs in the third row from the end.

6. Wrap a single band two times across the left and middle pegs in the fourth row from the end. Do the same for the fifth and sixth rows from the end.

7. Either on your loom or using your hook, make a white single-loop chain five bands long for your dog's tail.

8. Thread the end loops of your tail onto your hook. Double-loop a single band and pull it tight between your hook and your finger. Thread the loops for your tail onto the double-looped band.

9. Attach the double-looped tail band to the left and middle pegs in the sixth row.

To Put It All Together:

1. Put your hook through a stitch

on the back of your dog's head piece, as
shown. Pull a single white band partway
through so the ends of the band hang off
the back of the face. Do the same on the
right side.

2. Attach both loops from the single
   bands onto the right and left pegs
   on the end of the loom. Turn your
   loom so the dog is facing you.

3. Pull the middle of the band across
   the first row off the middle peg.

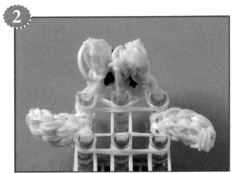

4. Starting at the peg closest to you
   on the left, begin looping your
   bands back. Loop the left column first,
   making sure to loop the diagonal band
   from the last peg back to the peg in the
   middle column. Then loop the bands in
   the right column, stopping after you loop
   the sixth peg. Loop the middle pegs next,
   stopping again after the sixth peg.

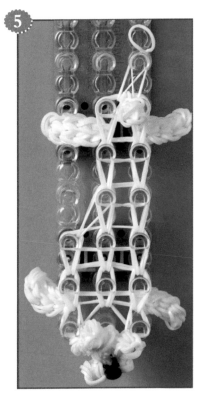

5. Pull your dog's tail toward you to move
   it out of the way, then loop your last
   two pegs. Then loop the band from the
   second-to-last peg on the right back to
   the last peg in the right column. Loop
   the single band from the last middle peg
   to the last peg in the right column.

6. Secure the loose loops on the final peg
   with a single band: pull the band through

the loops, then pull one end of the band through the other and pull it tight.

7. Remove your dog from the loom. Use your fingers to neaten up the bands and your hook to tuck in any leftover loops. Use your fingers to slide two red bands around your dog's neck for a collar.

SPiDeR

This creepy crawly spider isn't too scary, and it's a cinch to put together! This little arachnid fits in your pocket, and it makes a terrific handmade Halloween decoration!

Difficulty level: **Easy**

You need:

1 loom • 1 hook • 1 c-clip • black bands • 2 red bands

Set up your loom offset with the middle column pulled one peg closer to you.

To Make the Legs:

1. Lay out a line of double bands up the left column, ending on the seventh peg for the short legs, and the tenth peg for the long legs, as shown. Wrap a black cap band onto the last peg three times.

2. Turn your loom around. Starting at the peg where you placed the cap band, loop your bands back to the pegs where they started.

3. Secure the loose bands with a c-clip for now and set aside.

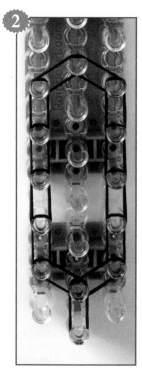

4. Make six total short legs and two total long legs in this way.

To Make the Body:

1. Attach two black bands to the first middle peg, then connect them to the next middle peg.

2. Starting on the second middle peg, lay out a long hexagon shape. Lay out the left side, then lay out the right side of the shape in the same way.

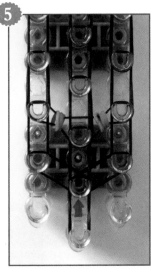

3. Lay out a line of double black bands up the middle of your hexagon.

4. Wrap two red bands around your hook three times. Thread your red bands onto a single black band. These will be your spider's eyes.

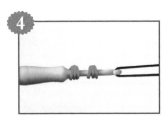

5. Attach your eye band to the third row of pegs, in a triangle shape.

6. Lay a single band in a triangle shape across the second, fourth, and fifth rows.

7. Wrap a cap band around the last middle peg three times.

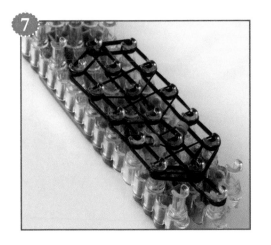

8. Add your spider legs: Remove the c-clip, and slide all four loose loops onto the pegs, as shown. Place the two long legs on the second pegs on the right and left.

9. Begin looping your bands back to where they started: Loop the closest middle peg first, then loop the left column, then the right. Loop the middle column last.

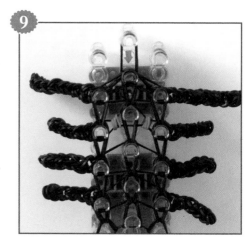

10. Finish your project by looping the single band from the second-to-last middle peg back to the last middle peg. Secure the loose loops with a c-clip or tie it off with a rubber band.

11. Remove your spider from your loom. Bend your spider's legs to make him stand!

PiG

Oink! Just like real pigs, this little piggy is smart: he can even stand up on his own! This project has a few pieces, but he's not too hard to put together!

Difficulty level: **Medium**

You need:

1 loom • 1 hook • pink, black, brown, and white bands

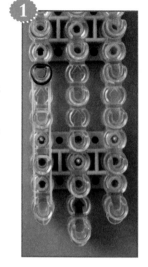

Set up your loom offset, with the center column pulled one closer to you and the arrow facing away.

1. Lay a line of pink bands down the left column, ending on the fourth peg. Wrap a black cap band around the fourth peg three times, then repeat with a second black cap band.

2. Turn your loom around and loop your bands back where they started. Repeat to make four legs for your pig.

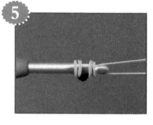

3. Using pink double bands, lay out a hexagon shape onto the loom. Lay out the left side then the right.

4. Lay a line of double pink bands down the center of your hexagon.

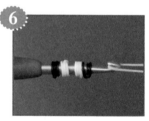

5. To make the snout, wrap a brown band around your hook three times, then thread it onto double pink bands. Put both ends of the pink bands onto your hook. Thread the pink bands and the brown band onto a single pink band. Set snout aside while you make the eyes.

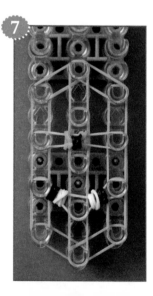

6. To make the eyes, wrap a black band around your hook three times. Do the same with a white band, then another white band, and finally another black band. Thread these onto a single pink band.

7. Place the single band with your snout onto the third row on the loom. Place the single band with your eye bands onto the second row in a triangle shape.

8. Wrap a pink band around your hook three times, then thread it onto a single pink band. Put both loops of the pink band onto your hook, then put them onto the first peg on the left. Repeat and place your second ear on the first right peg.

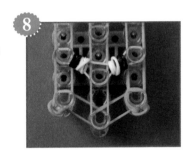

9. Wrap a pink band around your hook two times. Attach it to the first pegs on the right and left. Repeat and place your band across the fourth row in a triangle shape. Place two pink bands onto the third row in a triangle shape.

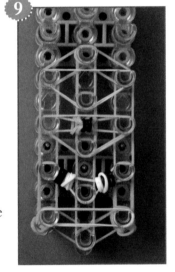

10. Turn your loom and loop your bands back to where they started. Loop the outside columns, then the center column. Pull a single pink band through the final loose loops: pull one end of the pink band through the other and pull it tight like a slipknot.

11. Remove your pig's face from the loom. Wrap a pink band around your hook twice, then slide it onto your pig's snout. Repeat with a second band.

12. Starting at the seventh middle peg from the end, lay a line of double pink bands down the center of your loom. Attach two pink bands to the seventh middle peg from the end, and connect them to the left; then repeat and connect them to the right. Lay a line of double bands down both outside columns.

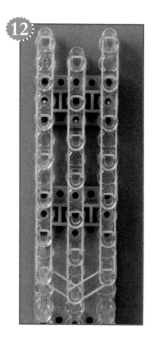

13. Place your pig's legs onto the corner pegs of your shape.

14. Place two bands across the seventh row from the end. Lay out double pink bands in a triangle shape across the remaining rows in your shape. Pull the triangle on the last pegs in front of the last middle peg.

15. Use your hook to pull a single pink band through the loops on the outside of your pig's face. Do this on both sides of the face.

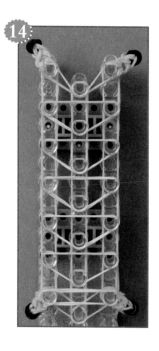

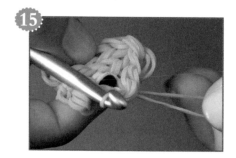

16. Place the loops on the outside pegs of the last row.

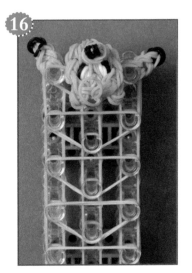

17. Turn your loom and loop your bands back to where they started. Tie off the last loose loops with a single pink band: pull one end of the band through the other to make a slipknot, then remove the pig from the loom.

BUNNY

Here comes Peter Rubberband-tail! This fluffy bunny can be made in a rainbow of colors. Make him as a festive springtime accessory or just about any time you need an extra bounce in your step.

Difficulty level: **Easy**

You need:

1 loom • 1 hook • purple, white, pink, and black bands

Set up your loom offset, with the middle column pulled toward you one peg.

To Make the Arms:

1. Lay out a line of double bands along the left column, ending on the fourth peg. Wrap a white cap band onto the fourth peg three times.

2. Turn your loom around. Loop your bands back to the pegs where they started.

3. Secure the loose loops from the final peg with your hook, or with a c-clip, and remove the arm from the loom. Set it aside. Repeat to make your bunny's second arm.

To Make the Head:

1. Lay double bands in a hexagon shape onto your loom as shown, first laying out the left side, then the right.

2. Lay double bands down the middle of your hexagon, ending on the third peg.

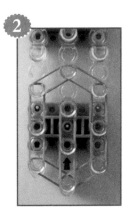

3. Wrap a pink band onto your hook three times. Thread it onto two purple bands, and attach the bands to the second and third pegs in the middle column. This will be your bunny's mouth.

4. Wrap two separate black bands onto your hook three times. Thread the bands onto two purple bands, and attach the bands to the second row, making sure the black bands are pushed to either side.

5. Wrap a single band twice across each the first and third rows, as shown.

To Make the Ears:

1. Wrap a purple band around your hook three times. Thread it onto two purple bands, then wrap a white band around your hook three times. Place the end of your two purple bands onto the hook behind the white band.

2. Continue to "knit" in this way, threading the loops from your hook onto double purple bands, then adding a white band to the hook before putting the other end of the purple double band onto the hook. Knit a chain three loops long.

3. Stretch a single purple band between your hook and your finger, and slide the loops off the hook, threading them onto the single band.

4. Place your bunny ear onto the first peg in the left column. Repeat to make your second ear, and place it onto the first peg in the right column.

To Make the Body:

1. Attach a single purple band to the fourth middle peg, and connect it to the left. Attach another single band, and connect it to the right.

2. Lay out purple double bands in a long hexagon shape, as you did for the head. Lay out the left side first, then the right.

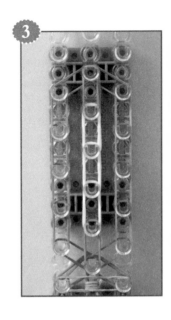

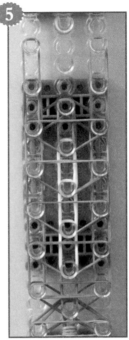

3. Lay a line of double bands down the middle of your body shape. Use purple bands for the first and last set of pegs and white bands in the middle.

4. Lay double bands down the right and left columns to make your bunny's legs.

5. Attach double bands to the fifth through the eighth rows in a triangle shape, as shown. Attach two purple bands to the fourth row.

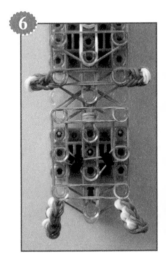

6. Place your bunny's arms on the right and left pegs in the fourth row.

To Make the Tail:

1. Wrap five separate purple bands onto your hook two times. Thread them onto a single purple band.

2. Place it onto the last peg in your body shape.

To Make the Feet:

1. Wrap a purple band onto your hook three times. Thread it onto two purple bands. Wrap a white band around the hook as you did for the ears, then put the other end of the purple bands back on the hook. Thread the purple and white bands onto two purple bands.

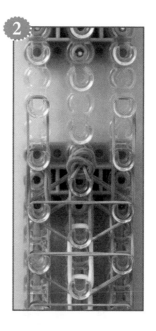

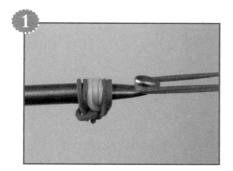

2. Place the foot onto the loom. Repeat for the second foot.

To Loop Your Bunny:

1. Turn your loom around. Loop your bunny's legs, then loop the middle peg with his tail. Loop the left side of the body shape, then the right, and then finally the middle column.

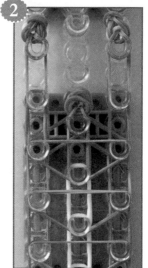

2. When you loop the middle "neck" peg, you should loop the middle peg first, then the one to the left, and, finally, the bands going to the right. Then finish looping the head shape as you did the body.

3. Secure the loose loops from the final peg with a c-clip or tie it off with a single band. Remove your bunny from the loom.

MEDUSA

Beware the terrifying and beautiful Greek Gorgon! Medusa was a mythological monster with live snakes for hair who could turn all those who stared at her to stone. Her name actually means "guardian," for her power to stop anyone in his tracks. We have shown how to make her wide dress using only one loom. If you have an extra loom, simply add one column on either side of her and lay out all the bands for the dress together. Now get rolling and make this super cool figure with all her slithering green snakes!

Difficulty level: **Medium**

You need:

1 loom • 1 hook • green, maroon, purple, red, black, and yellow bands

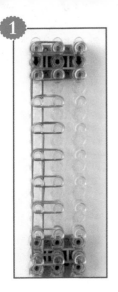

Set up your loom square so that all the columns are even. All the bands will be double bands, unless otherwise mentioned.

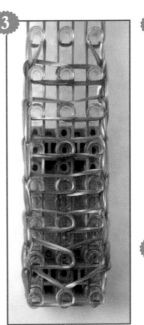

1. Lay out a line of purple double bands in the far left column and perpendicular bands along each row. This will be part of her dress. Loop these bands back, starting from the bottom (treat the last band as a cap band).

2. Repeat this process on the opposite column on the right side of the loom, with the perpendicular bands going left. Set these aside, and lay out her head and body, as shown.

3. Attach the purple bands that you set aside to the sides of the loom to widen her dress.

4. Place three separate crossover bands onto her torso (rows 4, 5, and 6 on the loom). To do this, wrap a single purple band on itself before stretching it across the loom. For the bottom crossover band, you will need to temporarily unhook the extra dress bands, attach the crossover band, and reattach the extra dress bands, as shown.

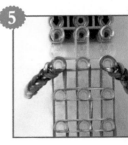

5. Make her arms by creating a chain of double bands using yellow, purple, and red bands and attach to the loom at her shoulders.

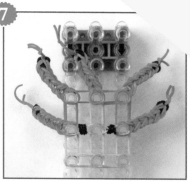

6. You are almost ready to loop your bands back, but first, scoot the bottom red bands to the inside of the outer columns, as shown. Now loop your bands back to the pegs where they started, beginning at the bottom of the loom. Once finished, carefully remove from the loom and set aside.

7. Lay out green and yellow bands for her face. Wrap two single black bands onto a hook and slide them onto a single yellow band that has been wrapped on itself. These will be the eyes; attach them to the middle of her face. Create six snakes for her hair by knitting chains made first of a black single band, followed by green double bands. Add knotted single red bands to the heads of the snakes, and snip the ends to look like their tongues. Attach these six snakes to her hair on the loom.

8. Attach Medusa's body to the bottom of her head. Starting from the bottom of her head, loop the bands back to the pegs where they started. Secure with an extra rubber band or a c-clip when you finish, and carefully remove from the loom.

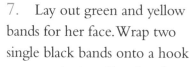

MERMAN

Check out what's under the sea! This cool merman is twenty thousand leagues of fun and is super simple to make. Once you have him made, make sure to pair him with your other sea creatures!

Difficulty level: **Easy**

You need:

1 loom • 1 hook • 3 different colors of bands

Set up your loom square so the three columns are all in an even line. All the bands will be double bands unless otherwise mentioned.

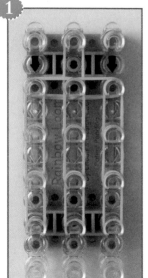

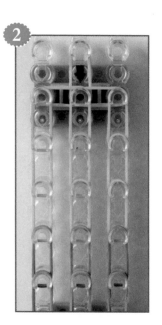

1. Begin by laying out the torso of the merman, as shown.

2. Change colors to start his fins, going all the way down the loom until you have done six rows. Close off the fin by bringing the bands to a point.

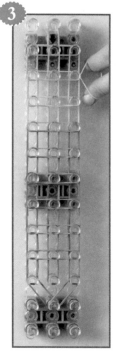

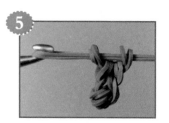

3. Lay out crossover bands to secure the body. These are single bands that are wrapped once on themselves before they are placed across the figure. You will have a total of eight crossover bands.

4. Create the split in the fins by wrapping a single band around your hook. Slide this onto a double band.

5. Repeat this until you have a whole fin. Make two fins total.

6. Attach both fins to the bottom center peg in the figure.

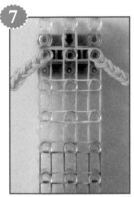

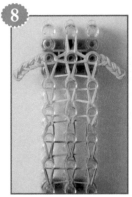

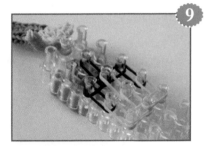

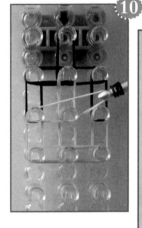

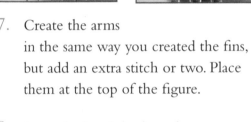

7. Create the arms in the same way you created the fins, but add an extra stitch or two. Place them at the top of the figure.

8. Loop the bands back to the pegs where they came from, starting with the fins at the bottom.

9. Set the body aside and create the face of the merman, as shown.

10. Wrap a band that is the same color as the merman's face on itself so that it is taut. Wrap two separate black bands onto a hook. Slide both of these bands onto the tight band, and attach it to the center of the merman's face.

11. Attach the body of the merman to the bottom of his face. Starting from this peg, loop the project back to the top of his head and secure before removing from the loom.

BUTTeRFLY

Turn those rubber band caterpillars into beautiful butterflies! This super cute project has a few moving parts, but it is very easy to assemble. Try making many of them in all sorts of colors for a kaleidoscope of butterflies!

Difficulty level: **Easy**

You need:

1 loom • 1 hook • 4 c-clips • purple, pink, white, and black bands

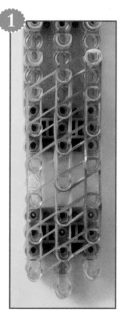

Set up your loom so that the center column is offset, with one peg closer to you and the arrow facing away. All bands are double bands unless otherwise mentioned.

1. For the first large wing, start from the left column and move right. Lay out a line of pink double bands, then rows of pink double bands to connect to the center column. Lay out a line of pink double bands in the center column, and then rows of purple double bands to connect to the right-hand column. Finally, lay out a line of purple double bands, securing the top peg with a white cap band.

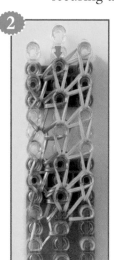

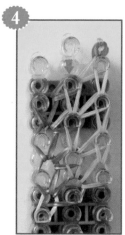
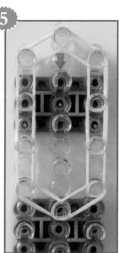

2. Turn the loom around and loop the bands back to the pegs where they started, beginning from the white cap band. Secure the top of the wing with a purple band and c-clip before removing from the loom and setting aside. The c-clips are temporary. Repeat these steps for the second large wing.

3. For the smaller wings, you will repeat the same process but with fewer bands.

4. Turn the loom around and begin from the white cap band as you loop

the project back. Secure with a purple band and c-clip, remove from the loom, and repeat for the second small wing.

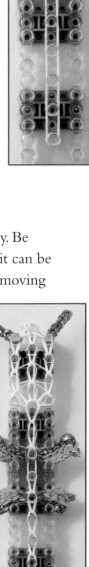

5. Set the wings aside and make the head of the butterfly using white double bands.

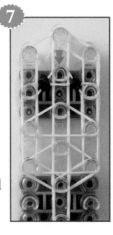

6. Lay out white double bands down the entire center column to create the body of the butterfly, ending with a cap band.

7. Attach crossover bands to the head as well as the eyes using a white band that has been threaded through two black knots.

8. Make two antennae by creating a chain of pink and purple double bands. Attach these and the wings to the loom, as shown. (Remove the c-clips before attaching the wings.)

9. Loop the project back, starting from the bottom of the body. Be careful while looping the areas where the wings connect—it can be tricky! Secure the top of the project with a c-clip before removing from the loom.

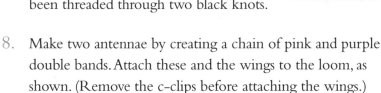

ALieN

This little green alien comes together faster than you can say "out of this world"! Make a bunch and start your own invasion!

Difficulty level: **Easy**

You need:

1 loom • 1 hook • green and black bands

1. Starting at the first middle peg, use double bands to lay a long hexagon shape onto the loom. Lay out the left side, then the right side.

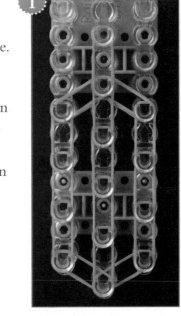

2. Lay a line of double bands up the center column, ending on the sixth peg. Using green double bands, lay a long hexagon shape onto the loom for the body. Lay out the left side, then the right side. Lay a line of double green bands down the middle of the body shape.

3. Wrap a green band around your hook three times. Use your hook to "knit" a chain two loops long with the green band on the end. Repeat to make another chain.

4. Thread both chains onto two green bands. Continue to use your hook to "knit" a chain five loops long with a fork at the end; this is your alien's leg. Repeat to make a second leg. Place the legs onto the two outside pegs in the

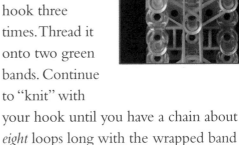

fourth row from the end.

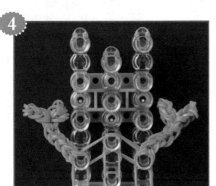

5. To make the arms, wrap a green band around your hook three times. Thread it onto two green bands. Continue to "knit" with

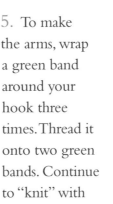

your hook until you have a chain about *eight* loops long with the wrapped band at the end. Repeat to make another chain the same length. Attach your arms to your alien's body shape.

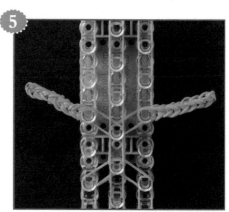

6. Wrap two separate black bands onto your hook. Thread them onto a single green band and attach it to the second row in a triangle shape. Make sure the eyes are pushed to each side.

7. Wrap a green band around your hook twice, then attach it to the third row on the loom in a triangle shape. Continue laying out triangle shapes down your alien's body, using single bands doubled over. You'll lay out six triangles total. Wrap a cap band around the last middle peg three times.

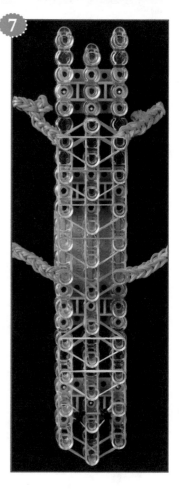

8. Starting at the last middle peg, loop your bands back where they started. Tie off the last loops with a single green band or use a c-clip.

PENGUIN

Hit the Antarctic with this waddling loom friend! This fun penguin will make for a happy addition to your loom zoo creatures and is a cinch to make! So bundle up and get working on this chill conqueror of the South Pole.

Difficulty level: **Easy**

You need:

1 loom • 1 hook • 1 c-clip • blue, black, white, dark orange, and light orange bands

Set up your loom square so that the columns are aligned evenly and the arrows are pointing toward you. All bands are double bands.

1. Lay out the penguin's head with black double bands, as shown.

2. Lay out a row of light orange double bands, followed by white double bands, as shown.

3. Knit two chains of black double bands for each of the arms. Attach to the shoulders of the penguin.

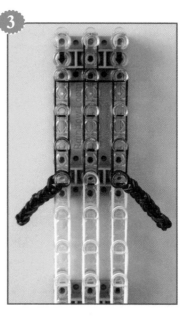

4. Make a beak by knitting a short chain of dark orange double bands (just two knots). Connect to the project using a black band. Add eyes by sliding knotted blue bands from your hook to a black band that has been wrapped once on itself so it is taut.

5. Attach white crossover bands to the body of the penguin. These will be double bands that are stretched across each set of pegs. Add feet by making more short

chains of black double bands and attaching them to the loom.

6. Starting from the feet, loop the bands back to the pegs where they started.

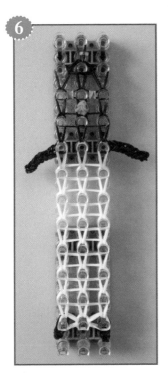

7. Attach a c-clip and gently remove from the loom.

CRAB

Make your day a little sunnier with this beach-dwelling creature, even on a snow day! Pay attention to the color changes to make a tie-dyed shell that's extra cool!

Difficulty level: **Easy**

You need:

1 loom • 1 hook • white, light orange, dark orange, and black bands

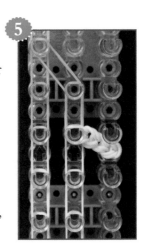

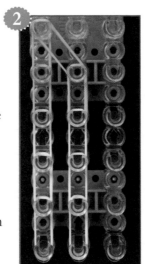

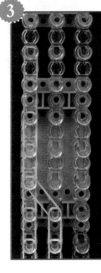

1. Lay a line of white double bands down the left and center columns, ending on the fourth peg.

2. Continue your line of double bands, using a white and a light orange band to connect the fifth and sixth pegs. Use light orange double bands to connect the sixth and seventh pegs on the left and for the diagonal band from the center peg to the left.

3. Continue your line of double bands up the left column, ending on the tenth peg. Use two light orange bands, then a light and a dark orange band for the next pegs. End with two sets of dark orange double bands. Wrap a dark orange cap band around the last peg three times.

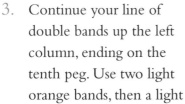

4. Wrap a white band onto your hook three times. Thread it onto two white bands. Use your hook to continue "knitting" a chain four loops long. Use a white and a light orange band for your last pair of bands.

5. Place your chain onto the loom on the middle peg right above the fork.

6. Wrap a white band around your hook twice, and place it over the left and middle pegs in

the fourth row. Repeat for the third and second row.

7. Turn your loom and begin looping your bands back to where they started. Put your hook through the last two loose loops and remove your crab's claw from the loom. Repeat steps 1 through 7 to make a second claw.

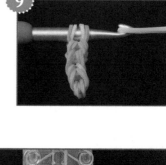

8. Attach two dark orange bands to the first middle peg, and connect it to the next middle peg. Starting on the second middle peg, lay out a long hexagon of dark orange double bands. Lay a line of dark orange double bands down the middle of your hexagon shape.

9. To make the legs, wrap a dark orange band onto your hook three times. Thread it onto two dark orange bands. Use your hook to "knit" a chain five loops long (not counting the first tripled band). Use dark orange for the first three loops, then use a light and a dark orange and use two light orange bands for the last loop.

10. Repeat to make six total legs. Attach your legs and your claw from earlier to the loom, as shown.

11. Wrap two separate black bands around your hook three times. Thread them onto a single dark orange band, and place the band onto the third row on your loom in a triangle shape. Make sure the black bands are pushed to the outside.

12. Turn your loom around and begin looping your bands back where they started. Secure the last two loose loops with a c-clip and remove your crab from the loom.

GiNGERBREAD MAN

Y um! This gingerbread man is cute enough to eat! But you probably shouldn't, because he is made of rubber bands.

Set up your loom square with the arrow facing away from you.

1. Lay double bands across the first row, moving from left to right. Lay a line of double bands up each column.

2. Attach double bands to the third peg on the left, and connect it to the next middle peg. Do the same on the right. Lay double bands across the fourth row, moving from left to right.

3. Attach two bands to the center peg in the fourth row, and connect it to the next middle peg. Lay a line of double bands down the outside columns, ending on the tenth peg.

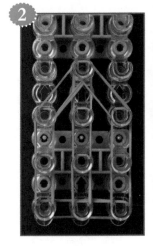

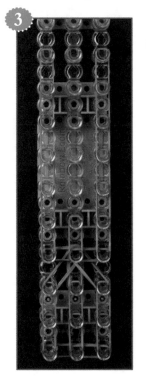

4. Wrap a green band around your hook three times, and thread it onto double brown bands. Lay it onto the loom above your last middle band. Repeat to make a second button, and place it above the first one, as shown.

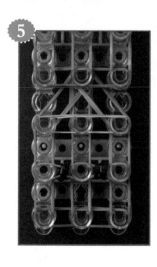

5. Wrap two separate black bands onto your hook three times and thread them onto two brown bands. Attach it to the second row on your loom.

6. Lay two pairs of double bands down the outside columns of your loom at the bottom of your gingerbread body shape. Wrap a cap band around each of the last pegs three times.

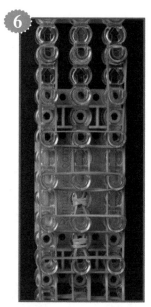

7. Use the bottom of your loom to make the arms: lay down two lines of double bands, as shown, and wrap a cap band around the last peg in each line three times. Loop your arm bands as usual.

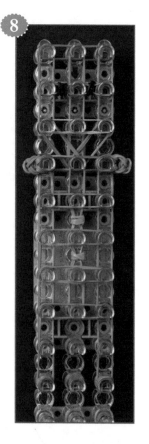

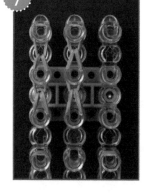

8. Remove the arms from the loom, and stack the loose loops onto the outside pegs in the fourth row.

9. Turn your loom around, and loop the outside columns of your gingerbread man all the way up to his neck. Pull the horizontal band between his legs so that it is not on the center peg.

10. Loop the middle column, then loop the head shape normally.

11. Remove your gingerbread man from the loom. Wrap a white band around your hook twice, then slide it around his ankle. Do this with the rest of his limbs.

STARFiSH

Hit the beach with this awesome starfish! Mix your colors to form one of the coolest underwater creatures in seas near and far. This project is super easy, and you can create a whole kingdom of them to decorate your room or bring swimming with you!

Difficulty level: **Easy**

You need:

1 loom • 1 hook • 2 colors of bands

Set up the loom so the center column is offset one peg away from you. All the bands will be double bands made of two different colors.

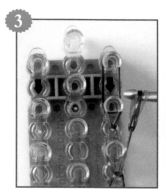

1. Lay out a series of six double bands in the far right column and one double band partway down the center column, as shown. Wrap a cap band on the bottom peg in the right column.

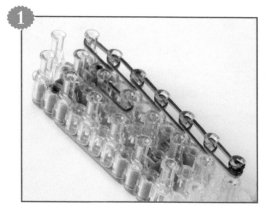

2. Starting from the bottom peg with the cap band, begin to loop the bands back to the pegs where they started. When you reach the peg near the center bands, loop diagonally across to the center bands.

3. Return to the right column and loop once more, then carry the looped bands from the center column over to this peg, as shown.

4. Carefully remove this from the loom and set aside. Create a total of five starfish arms.

5. Place the starfish arms on the loom, using the loops to spread between pegs.

6. Continue in a circular fashion around the loom. There will be one area that will not have an arm. Make a figure eight with a double band and attach to this area to connect the sides of the starfish.

7. Starting from the "two o'clock" peg, lay out six double bands from the center peg around the circle. The double bands should be the same color.

8. From the bands that you laid down last, loop these bands back, as shown.

9. Next, loop the bands going around the circumference of the starfish. Secure a band at the top of the project and carefully remove from the loom.

Loom Magic!

25 Awesome, Never-Before-Seen Designs for an Amazing Rainbow of Projects

by John McCann &
Becky Thomas

This book includes twenty-five new rubber band loom projects, including bracelets, sports-themed charms, key rings, pendants, and even a working slingshot. New crafters and dedicated fans will enjoy creating a wide variety of projects in this collection, including:

- Cellphone Case
- Daisy Chain Bracelet
- Watch Band
- Octo Bracelet
- Blooming Beaded Bracelet
- Sports Fan Key Chain
- Matching Barrettes
- Pencil Topper
- Bling Ring
- Nunchuks
- Rocker Cuff Bracelet
- Snowman Ornament
- And many more!

$12.95 Hardcover • 978-1-62914-334-7